Rock Hound's
LOGBOOK & JOURNAL

by Dan R. Lynch

Adventure Publications, Inc.
Cambridge, MN

DEDICATION

To Julie Kirsch, for her endless love and patience.

And to my parents.

ACKNOWLEDGMENTS

Thanks to the following for providing specimens and/or information:
George Robinson Ph.D., Robert Weikert, George Godas and John Perona

Photography by Dan R. Lynch

Edited by Brett Ortler

Cover and book design by Jonathan Norberg

10 9 8 7 6 5 4 3 2 1

Copyright 2010 by Dan R. Lynch
Published by Adventure Publications, Inc.
820 Cleveland St. S
Cambridge, MN 55008
1-800-678-7006
www.adventurepublications.net
All rights reserved

ISBN-13: 978-1-59193-260-4
ISBN-10: 1-59193-260-2

Table of Contents

Introduction 4

Rockhounding Tips and Advice 4

The Hazards of Rockhounding 9

Photography 11

How to Use This Book 12

Logbook 14

Notes 98

Checklist 108

Glossary 113

Recommended Reading 119

About the Author 120

Introduction

For many people, the term "rock hound" conjures up visions of grandfathers who keep dusty rock collections in their basements. For others, it might be the "Rocky the Rockhound" cartoon that depicts a dog—complete with miner's helmet and pickaxe—drooling over gems laid out in front of him. In reality, rock hounds are hobbyists of any age who are passionate about examining, finding, buying and displaying rocks and minerals. If you've ever picked up a stone and admired it for its beauty or color, you can consider yourself a rock hound as well.

There are over 4,000 minerals known today, with more being identified each year. The vast majority are extremely rare minerals that were only found once in a specific location, and as very tiny crystals. When a new mineral is found, the only thing more important than its identity is the location where it was found. When we know where a mineral came from, it offers a window into the geological history of the area and how its rocks and minerals came to be. While most rock hounds will never find a new, unknown mineral, it is as important for amateur rock hounds to take careful notes of specimen locations as it is for the professional. You, your family, and your fellow rock hounds will always value the knowledge of a specific specimen's location because it will signify one stop on your rockhounding journey.

Within the pages of this book are blank entries for rock hounds of all experience levels to record their mineral finds, as well as some advice, tips and a checklist. Treat this book as a journal for your rockhounding adventures—write in it, draw in it and get it dirty. Soon, it will have as much character as your collection.

Rockhounding Tips and Advice

When it comes to rockhounding, there are two schools of thought. Much like birdwatchers, there are those who seek out rock formations and mineral outcroppings in their natural setting merely to observe and photograph them. Well-read hobbyists take this more naturalistic approach to learn how different rocks and minerals relate to each other and also about the geology of an entire region. At the other end of the spectrum, there are rock hounds who seek to add the finest rock and mineral specimens to their collections and use a host of equipment to do so. Whatever your approach, this logbook was designed with all rock hounds in mind.

No rock hound goes to a site and immediately finds a gem. The key to successful hunting is perseverance—it may take hours of examining rock

PRIVATE AND PROTECTED AREAS

As a rock hound, it is your responsibility to know where you can and cannot collect. In many areas of the United States it's illegal to collect anything; this includes the many National Parks and National Monuments, and State Parks, among other areas. Collecting on private land without permission is also illegal. If you're caught collecting on protected land, prepare yourself for a large fine. And if an angry landowner finds you digging in his field, the penalty may be worse than just a few dollars. All rock hounds are encouraged to respect the boundaries of national and state parks so that generations to come may enjoy the untouched and uncollected natural beauty and significance of these areas. When it comes to private land, it is no one's fault but your own if you are caught trespassing without having first obtained permission from the landowner.

It can sometimes be difficult to determine if an area is closed to collecting. National and state parks are clearly marked on most maps, but private land is another story. "No trespassing" signs are obviously a big clue, though not all property is posted. You might start by asking around town—even gas station clerks might know where the locals hunt rocks. If there is a local rock shop, they might also have great information on where hunting is allowed or if certain areas are off-limits. Local geologists can also be helpful. If the area appears to be privately owned, seek out the owner to gain permission.

In some places in the US, especially in the western states, you must be aware of claimed land. When a plot of land has been claimed, it means that someone has paid for the rights to collect there, often because rare or valuable minerals such as gold are there. No one else is allowed upon the claim without permission, and it therefore should be considered off-limits. Most claims are small areas, clearly marked with stakes and signs. Panning for gold in a river that sits on someone's property or land claim can get you arrested or, in extreme cases, shot at by the landowner. These rockhounding "horror stories" are reminders that knowing where you are collecting has never been more important.

formations or walking miles of beach before finding even an average-quality specimen. At times it feels like "all work and no play," but once you find that breathtaking crystal, it suddenly seems worth the trouble.

There is more to rockhounding than just going out and picking up rocks. Like any hobby or profession, you will learn a lot of "insider" information in the process. Once you discover the ins-and-outs of the trade, you'll begin to develop tips and tricks of your own.

BE PREPARED

Undertaking a rockhounding expedition without the right equipment or knowledge of the area will only result in wasted time and effort. Researching an area's geology before you leave home is an essential first step. Whether you plan on taking specimens home with you or are merely setting out to take photos, noting if the site consists of igneous, sedimentary, or metamorphic rocks is critical for success.

Before you set out on your journey, let others know where you will be and when you expect to return. It is also essential to be aware of a territory's rules and regulations and to understand them completely before visiting. In addition, whether you have permission to collect or if you're just planning on observing an area's geology, you may want to bring the following with you:

1. Adequate food and water—especially in hot weather or desert regions where dehydration is a real danger

2. Sunglasses, hat and sunblock, no matter what the weather

3. First-aid kit

4. Thick leather gloves and knee pads—these are even more important in areas with lots of jagged, sharp rocks

5. Durable clothes that can shed rain or block the sun

6. GPS (global positioning system) device for finding your way to a collecting site, marking the position of a new find, and marking the location of your vehicle so that you do not get lost

7. Field guide for determining where to look, what to look for, and how to identify various rocks and minerals

If you're planning to collect from areas where it's allowed, consider packing these items too:

1. Extra water for rinsing dust from specimens

2. Dust mask or respirator—critical if you plan on collecting minerals that create harmful dust, such as chrysotile serpentine, a variety of asbestos

3. Waders or boots if you plan on searching in rivers or lakes

4. Bucket or other container with sturdy handles for carrying specimens home

5. Rock hammer (not a nail hammer) and chisel if you plan on breaking rocks to find minerals contained inside

6. Pens, paper and tape for labeling specimens and taking notes

LABELING AND CLEANING SPECIMENS

If you decide to collect specimens from areas where it is allowed, you'll want to label them as soon as possible so that you don't forget what they are or where they came from. Then you'll likely want to clean some of your samples—the bright, shiny rocks and minerals you find in shops didn't start off that way, and neither will your specimens. Very delicate crystals or soft minerals should be left just as they are, as cleaning them will cause them more harm than good. More durable minerals should be rinsed with water. Soap can also be used if there is stubborn mud or stains on the specimen, but be sure to rinse thoroughly or soak overnight to eliminate any chance of leftover soap residue. However, be aware that some minerals (such as halite and chalcanthite) dissolve in water, so do some research beforehand. Many experienced rock hounds suggest using acids to clean minerals; amateurs should not attempt this process. While certain acids do clean stains from crystals (even stains deep within the specimen), acids can be dangerous if handled improperly. Even the fumes emitted by most acids can be hazardous. In addition, some acids will dissolve minerals and destroy them—placing a piece of calcite in vinegar is a good illustration of this process. In short, leave acid cleaning to the professionals and stick to soap, water and patience.

STORAGE TIPS

If you are collecting, you'll need to consider how you'll be storing and displaying the specimens. There are many methods available, but before you start arranging specimens on your shelves, you should first review how much space you have for your collection. If you live in a one-bedroom apartment, for example, you likely won't have room for a large collection and may want to keep only small specimens that are easier to store. But no matter how much space you have, keep in mind that space is always limited and that large specimens are much more difficult to move around. Collect within your means—don't take home more than you can handle.

There are six primary specimen sizes that you'll commonly read or hear about as you build your collection: micromounts, microminerals, thumbnails, miniatures, small cabinet minerals (also called palm-sized) and cabinet-sized specimens. Micromounts are tiny specimens that measure less than ¼ inch across. Many micromounts are displayed in small plastic boxes or, as for extremely small samples, glued to the tip of a needle. As tiny as micromounts can be, they often display perfect crystals when viewed under a microscope, and at such a small size, many fit in a small space. Microminerals are slightly larger than micromounts and will fit into a hinged plastic box measuring 1⅛ inches across and ⅞ inch tall. These tiny mineral specimens are similar to micromounts but often have a small amount of matrix, or base rock, attached. The most popular small-sized minerals are thumbnails, which fit into a 1¼-inch cube hinged plastic box, also called a "perky box." Thumbnails are the most practical size for smaller collections and many rock hounds have a prized collection of "perky box minerals." A miniature will fit into an oversized perky box measuring 2½ inches wide and 1¼ inches tall. Small cabinet minerals are about 3 or 4 inches across and can be displayed on a shelf or in a cabinet without a box protecting them. Small cabinet minerals are also often referred to as "palm-sized." Finally, cabinet-sized specimens are 5 to 10 inches across, making them ideal for larger shelf displays. Whatever size you choose to collect and display, be sure to keep your specimens clearly labeled so that you know what each specimen is and where it came from.

The photo below shows three specimens mounted and labeled in hinged plastic boxes. On the left is a micromineral, a thumbnail in a perky box is in the middle, and a miniature is on the right. A quarter is provided for reference.

SPECIALIZATION

Many people are often surprised to see that some life-long rock hounds' collections are rather small. This is generally because their collection was specialized and they sought only their favorite minerals, the finest specimens, or only saved minerals from their favorite collecting site.

Maybe the native elements, such as copper, gold and sulfur, are what draw you; perhaps it's fine crystals of quartz from all over the country or agates only from your hometown. Whatever your favorites are, consider making them your specialization. A small collection of world-class quartz crystals can be equally as impressive as a very large collection of assorted minerals. And in a few years' time, you could even be regarded as an expert on the kinds of minerals in which you specialize.

The Hazards of Rockhounding

One of the most overlooked aspects of rockhounding is that it can be a dangerous hobby. The dangers may not always be obvious, but when you begin climbing large piles of sharp broken rock, collecting radioactive minerals, or digging into hills where angry animals make their homes, you'll soon learn the perils of searching for minerals.

ABANDONED MINES

Minnesota's iron mines, Arizona and Michigan's copper mines, the coal quarries of Pennsylvania, and the uranium prospects in Colorado are just a few examples of the United States' rich history in mining. World-class mineral specimens have—and still do—come from these types of operations. But for each mine still being worked today, there are thousands more mines that have been closed or abandoned. It's unlikely that you would ever come across an unrestricted mine entrance, no matter how old; however, if you do, you should never enter! It may be tempting to see the inside of a dilapidated mine shaft or climb down into an abandoned quarry, but these are some of the most dangerous places a rock hound can be. Years of disrepair and neglect often cause the walls and supporting beams of mines or quarries to decay and make them liable to collapse when disturbed.

Animals, such as bears and bats, can also make abandoned mines their homes. And one of the least known dangers is the most deadly: Dangerous gases can build up in old mine shafts and too often people suffocate from venturing where they shouldn't.

MINE DUMPS AND ROCKSLIDES

Mine dumps, also called overburden piles, consist of the unwanted rock produced when a mine shaft is dug. These enormous piles are favored by collectors because of the fine specimens that can be found within. However, careless digging or climbing can easily cause an avalanche of hundreds of pounds of jagged rock to crash onto everything below. Similarly, the rock walls of quarries and gravel pits are generally very unstable, and climbing the cliffs is unwise. In many gravel pits, windy days will cause rocks to fall from the cliff walls, often causing a rockslide on their way down. The author has spent many hours listening to the eerie sound of spontaneously falling rocks behind him as he collected agates in gravel quarries.

WILDLIFE

Other hazards to be aware of include plant and animal life. In desert climates, you'd regret running into the spines of a cactus just because you were walking with your eyes to the ground. And if you carelessly overturn boulders, a coiled rattlesnake or angry scorpion may be the only "gem" you find. In the northern forests, a defensive mother bear protecting her cubs may be found just beyond where you're standing. Before you venture into the wilderness, consider buying a field guide to learn which plants and animals to avoid.

POTENTIALLY DANGEROUS ROCKS AND MINERALS

When it comes to the hazards of rockhounding, environmental dangers aren't the only concern. Sometimes the minerals themselves prove to be dangerous. More often than not, the health risks are well disguised and the unwitting rock hound can easily bring harmful minerals into his or her home. Some elements are poisonous and are contained within several collectible minerals. Lead, arsenic and mercury are three such elements and are present in galena, realgar and cinnabar, respectively. You should limit the amount of time spent handling these minerals and wash your hands thoroughly afterwards, or wear a pair of gloves to prevent overexposure to these toxic elements. If you find some specimens of an interesting, unknown mineral while in the field and can't research their identity until you've returned home, treat them with caution and handle them with gloves until you know otherwise.

The radioactive elements, including uranium and thorium, are another major hazard of rockhounding. Radioactivity can be thought of as an invisible, cancer-causing poison that radiates outward from its source, penetrating metal, wood and skin. Minerals containing these elements will be radioactive as well and great caution should be taken when collecting them. Generally speaking, very small amounts of radioactive minerals are safe to collect when stored away from food, water and the living areas of your home. The larger the specimen, however, the greater the radioactive energy and danger. Luckily, it would be unlikely for an amateur collector to accidentally pick up a strongly radioactive specimen as they are generally quite uncommon.

Finally, some minerals present an inhalation danger and are able to cause lung cancer. These minerals are known as asbestos. The term "asbestos" doesn't apply to any particular mineral, but rather a varied group of minerals that can form in masses of thin, flexible fibers. These fibrous minerals are renowned for their fire-resistant properties, but are notorious for their adverse health effects when inhaled. And they can be very easy to inhale; the flexible fibers can be as fine as human hair and small fragments easily become airborne. When collecting asbestos minerals, or collecting in an area known to contain asbestos, a respirator or dust mask is critical.

Throughout this book, minerals that pose a radioactivity danger are marked with a radioactivity symbol (☢). Those that are potentially dangerous because of toxic elements or that pose inhalation dangers are marked with an exclamation point (⚠). As with most aspects of rockhounding, research and awareness are the watchwords when dealing with hazardous minerals. There is no better defense than to simply know what you are collecting and its potential dangers.

Photography

Each of the photos in this logbook is a close-up look at the elaborate beauty found in minerals of all varieties. Even "ugly" specimens have something interesting to offer the rock hound—you'll just need a microscope, or in this case, a macro camera lens. Nothing in the photos has been edited or adjusted to change the minerals, and the actual specimens appear just as they do here. Each photo is paired with a caption that tells the name of the mineral as well as some brief information. The note in each caption about "width of view" refers to how the size of the image relates to the size of the specimen. For example, "Width of view: 5 mm" means that the width of the image, from left to right, measures only 5 millimeters across the actual specimen.

Taking photos like these takes a great deal of equipment, but even those rock hounds with a simple snapshot camera can take great mineral photos. Reducing glare via use of circular light polarizers and controlled lighting, and a background that is not-distracting are key. Use of computer programs can help remove unwanted dust spots and shadows, but you should always try to represent the mineral's true beauty and not tamper with the image's color. Let the specimen's natural beauty speak for itself—altering the image won't elicit any praise from your fellow rock hounds.

How to Use This Book

PURPOSE

This logbook is intended as a way to catalog your mineral-finding adventures. Since most collectors' "rock collections" actually consist of minerals, not rocks, the entries in this book are devoted to minerals. In many ways, the 116 minerals contained within this log can be thought of as a "wish list" of United States minerals, as they are the most common, most important and most desired minerals in the country. Completing this book by finding each mineral yourself would be a great feat, worthy of praise from even the most accomplished rock hounds. However, you can make entries for purchased minerals as well.

You'll need a rock and mineral field guide to identify your finds before they can be recorded. Even after learning all about an area's minerals, you may still agonize over the identity of a particular specimen, but that's part of the fun of rockhounding.

ORGANIZATION

The minerals in this logbook are listed alphabetically so that you can easily find a mineral's entry after you've identified your find. Most are given a single entry in which to record one specimen, but very common and important minerals are given several entries since you are likely to find them many times in multiple states. Groups of closely related minerals, such as the mica family, are listed as an entire group. This is because these groups contain several minerals that are all very similar in regards to both their appearances and chemical compositions and distinguishing one group member from another can be difficult for even experienced rock hounds.

MAKING ENTRIES

When recording a find, be as specific as possible. Write down everything you know about where you found it, including the state, county, and nearest town. If you have a global positioning system (GPS) device, record the exact coordinates of the collecting site to pinpoint the location for future reference. Any other information regarding the find can be valuable as well—minerals surrounding the specimen and the kind of rock it was found in, for example, are worthy of note. There is a "notes" section in the back of the book for additional writing space. If you decide to collect specimens, it would be wise to begin some kind of numbering system to keep your collection organized. The system could be as complex as you'd like, but simply labeling a specimen with a number and then writing the same number on the corresponding logbook entry would work well. A sample entry is included on the following page.

Orpiment with quartz

The unmistakable, lustrous orange-yellow crystals of orpiment are extremely soft and flexible, but easily turn to dust as they weather. Orpiment has been used as a yellow pigment for centuries, though its use is discouraged today because of orpiment's high arsenic content. (Width of view: 4 mm)

Magnetite HARDNESS: 5.5-6.5 STREAK: black RARITY: common

A magnet will stick to this widespread iron ore. Vermont, New York, New Mexico, Utah and California have produced well-crystallized specimens.

DATE: December 11, 2009

LOCATION: Flood Bay, Lake Superior shoreline, Two Harbors, Lake County, Minnesota

GPS COORDINATES: N92° 25.5' W24° 15.6'

NOTES: Specimen #072, found on lakeshore in black gravel and sand, about 1/2 mile south of the parking lot.

Malachite HARDNESS: 3.5-4 STREAK: light green RARITY: uncommon

Frequently found with azurite, malachite specimens are most famous from Arizona, but also come from California and Colorado.

DATE:

LOCATION:

GPS COORDINATES:

NOTES:

Manganite HARDNESS: 3.5-4 STREAK: reddish brown to black RARITY: uncommon

Named for its manganese content, excellent manganite specimens come from Virginia, Georgia, Michigan and Arizona.

DATE:

LOCATION:

GPS COORDINATES:

NOTES:

Lake Superior Agate

Not a traditional agate by any means, this polished Lake Superior specimen exhibits a strange interplay of tube and stalactite structures. Iron and its ores are most often responsible for the strange formations and colors present in Minnesota's agates. (Width of view: 17 mm)

Adamite HARDNESS: 3.5 STREAK: white RARITY: uncommon

These yellow zinc-based crystals are found in the Southwest, particularly Nevada, Utah and California.

DATE:

LOCATION:

GPS COORDINATES:

NOTES:

Andalusite HARDNESS: 7.5 STREAK: colorless RARITY: common

This primarily metamorphic mineral is found all over the US, but fine specimens come from Maine, Massachusetts, Arizona, California and Washington.

DATE:

LOCATION:

GPS COORDINATES:

NOTES:

Anglesite ⚠ HARDNESS: 2.5-3 STREAK: white to gray RARITY: uncommon

Fantastic examples of anglesite's white, lustrous crystals come from Pennsylvania, Colorado, Arizona, Nevada and Idaho.

DATE:

LOCATION:

GPS COORDINATES:

NOTES:

Azurite on psilomelane

Azurite is an easily identified mineral that is readily obtainable because of its sought-after color and numerous crystal habits (forms). In this specimen, blade-like crystals in circular groupings form beautiful rosettes, each topped with tiny flecks of green malachite. (Width of view: 11 mm)

Anhydrite **HARDNESS:** 3-3.5 **STREAK:** white to gray **RARITY:** common

When gypsum loses water, it becomes anhydrite, which is widespread throughout the US. Fine crystals are found in Arizona, Texas, Louisiana and New Jersey.

DATE:

LOCATION:

GPS COORDINATES:

NOTES:

Apatite **HARDNESS:** 5 **STREAK:** white **RARITY:** common

Beautiful specimens of this common phosphorus-bearing mineral come from California, North Carolina, Virginia and Massachusetts.

DATE:

LOCATION:

GPS COORDINATES:

NOTES:

Apophyllite **HARDNESS:** 4.5-5 **STREAK:** white **RARITY:** uncommon

High quality glassy crystals of apophyllite are well known from New Jersey, Pennsylvania, Virginia and Washington.

DATE:

LOCATION:

GPS COORDINATES:

NOTES:

Brochantite

The delicate needles of brochantite, one of Arizona's many collectible copper minerals, are pictured here lining a cavity in limonite. The emerald-green crystals are easily crushed by mishandling, but that doesn't stop collectors from buying fine specimens at high prices. (Width of view: 4 mm)

Aragonite **HARDNESS:** 3.5-4 **STREAK:** white **RARITY:** common

This cousin of calcite is common in every state, particularly in the Northeast and the Southwest. Fine examples are found in Arizona, New Mexico and Pennsylvania.

DATE:

LOCATION:

GPS COORDINATES:

NOTES:

Arsenopyrite **HARDNESS:** 5.5-6 **STREAK:** white **RARITY:** uncommon

Arsenopyrite is an important ore of arsenic and has come from Maine, New York, Colorado, Washington and Alaska.

DATE:

LOCATION:

GPS COORDINATES:

NOTES:

Augite **HARDNESS:** 5-6 **STREAK:** greenish **RARITY:** very common

Fine examples of this common pyroxene-group member are found in New York, South Carolina, Arizona and Oregon.

DATE:

LOCATION:

GPS COORDINATES:

NOTES:

"Binghamite," a variety of quartz

"Binghamite" is actually a form of quartz that has replaced fibrous iron ores, primarily goethite. It only comes from Minnesota's iron ranges and fetches high prices when polished. This specimen shows two cracks in the stone that were later filled with yellow, iron-stained quartz. (Width of view: 15 mm)

Aurichalcite HARDNESS: 1-2 STREAK: pale greenish to blue RARITY: uncommon

These zinc- and copper-rich blue crystals are most famous from Colorado, Utah, Arizona and California.

DATE:

LOCATION:

GPS COORDINATES:

NOTES:

Autunite ☢ HARDNESS: 2-2.5 STREAK: yellow RARITY: uncommon

This radioactive uranium-based mineral primarily comes from New Hampshire, North Carolina, Colorado and Washington.

DATE:

LOCATION:

GPS COORDINATES:

NOTES:

Azurite HARDNESS: 3.5-4 STREAK: blue RARITY: uncommon

Deep blue azurite commonly forms alongside malachite throughout the western US, particularly in Idaho, Utah, Arizona, Alaska and Washington.

DATE:

LOCATION:

GPS COORDINATES:

NOTES:

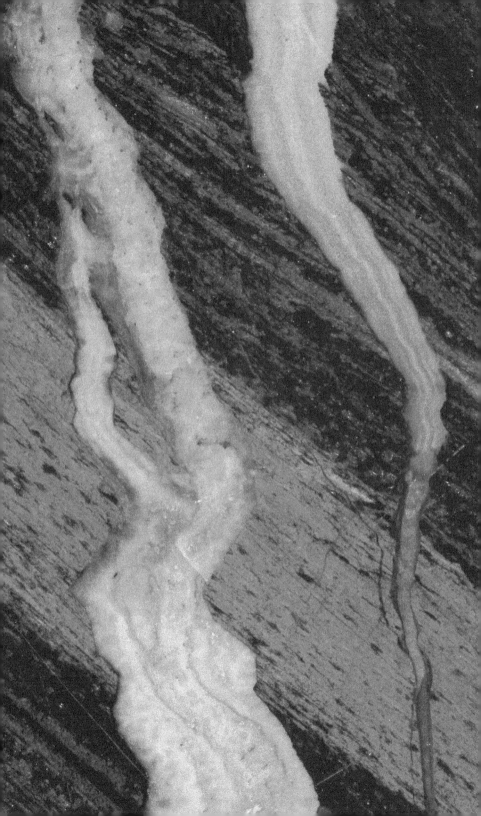

Prehnite with copper and chlorite inclusions

This polished portion of prehnite encases swirls of native copper and green chlorite. The prehnite itself is colorless or white, but appears orange and pink due to the pure, untarnished copper. Specimens like this are often found on Michigan's Lake Superior shoreline. (Width of view: 6 mm)

Barite HARDNESS: 3-3.5 STREAK: white RARITY: very common

Blade-like crystals of this common, heavy mineral are found everywhere, but particularly in South Dakota, Colorado, Arizona and California.

DATE:

LOCATION:

GPS COORDINATES:

NOTES:

Benitoite HARDNESS: 6-6.5 STREAK: colorless RARITY: rare

Beautiful blue, triangular crystals of benitoite only come from San Benito County, California

DATE:

LOCATION:

GPS COORDINATES:

NOTES:

Beryl HARDNESS: 7.5-8 STREAK: colorless RARITY: uncommon

Maine, South Dakota, Colorado, Idaho and Nevada all produce fine crystals of beryl, including emeralds and aquamarines.

DATE:

LOCATION:

GPS COORDINATES:

NOTES:

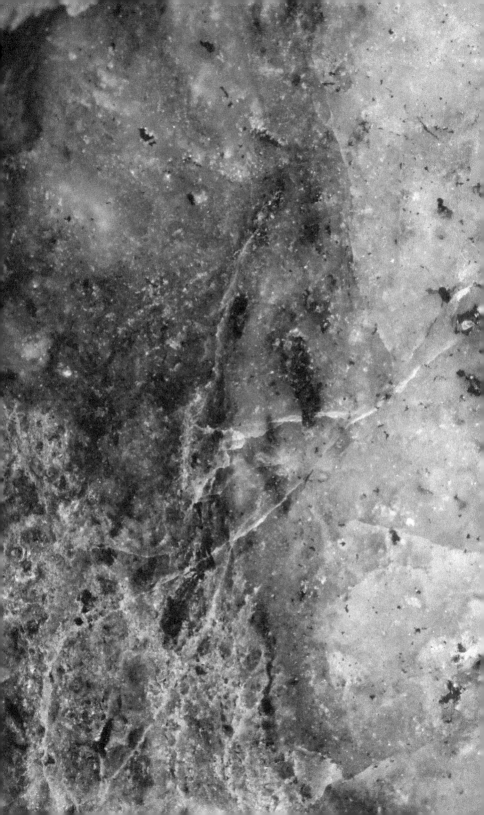

Chrysocolla on malachite

Balls of chrysocolla measuring only a quarter of an inch across grow on a crust of malachite in this specimen from Arizona. Green copper minerals occur together very often and can be difficult to tell apart. (Width of view: 6 mm)

Bornite **HARDNESS:** 3 **STREAK:** grayish black **RARITY:** uncommon

Often called "peacock ore," nice specimens of bornite can be found in Alaska, Oregon, Arizona, Montana and Virginia.

DATE:

LOCATION:

GPS COORDINATES:

NOTES:

Brochantite **HARDNESS:** 3.5-4 **STREAK:** pale green **RARITY:** rare

Tiny needle-like crystals of rich green color are found in Arizona, Colorado and Utah.

DATE:

LOCATION:

GPS COORDINATES:

NOTES:

Calcite **HARDNESS:** 3 **STREAK:** white **RARITY:** very common

Calcite is an extremely common and very important mineral, found in every state.

DATE:

LOCATION:

GPS COORDINATES:

NOTES:

Jarosite

If these yellow jarosite crystals look tiny, it's because they are. The largest crystals pictured here are no more than 0.17 mm across. Iron-bearing jarosite isn't found in large amounts, but is quite widespread across the US. (Width of view: 7 mm)

Calcite *(continued)* **HARDNESS:** 3 **STREAK:** white **RARITY:** very common

Some of the finest calcite specimens come from Michigan, Iowa, Missouri, Arkansas, Kansas and Washington.

DATE:

LOCATION:

GPS COORDINATES:

NOTES:

DATE:

LOCATION:

GPS COORDINATES:

NOTES:

Cassiterite **HARDNESS:** 6-7 **STREAK:** light brown–nearly white **RARITY:** uncommon

This important ore of tin is primarily found in Maine, North Carolina, Virginia, California, Washington and Alaska.

DATE:

LOCATION:

GPS COORDINATES:

NOTES:

Hübnerite

Tiny red blades of hübnerite, a member of the tungsten-rich wolframite series, form a mosaic in this specimen from Colorado. These flat, thin, striated crystals are fairly easy to identify—if you're lucky enough to find them. (Width of view: 5 mm)

Celestine HARDNESS: 3-3.5 STREAK: white RARITY: uncommon

Beautiful crystals of this light-blue mineral are found in California, Michigan, Ohio, Pennsylvania and New York.

DATE:

LOCATION:

GPS COORDINATES:

NOTES:

Cerussite ⚠ HARDNESS: 3-3.5 STREAK: white RARITY: common

Fine examples of this lead mineral's white, needle-like crystals are found in California, Arizona, Utah and Pennsylvania.

DATE:

LOCATION:

GPS COORDINATES:

NOTES:

Chalcanthite ⚠ HARDNESS: 2.5 STREAK: white RARITY: uncommon

This bright blue copper mineral is found in the Southwest, particularly in Arizona, Nevada, Utah and Colorado.

DATE:

LOCATION:

GPS COORDINATES:

NOTES:

Cyanotrichite

Cyanotrichite's name stems from the Greek words for "blue" and "hair," which, as anyone can see, is an apt description. The tiny needle-like crystals are rare in the US and their delicate nature makes them difficult to collect. (Width of view: 4 mm)

Chalcedony
HARDNESS: 7 **STREAK:** white **RARITY:** very common

A variety of microcrystalline quartz, chalcedony is common in many states, particularly Arizona. A highly desirable form is agate, which is banded chalcedony and is found in Minnesota and Michigan.

DATE:

LOCATION:

GPS COORDINATES:

NOTES:

DATE:

LOCATION:

GPS COORDINATES:

NOTES:

Chalcocite
HARDNESS: 2.5-3 **STREAK:** dark gray to black **RARITY:** common

Large amounts of this important ore of copper are found in Connecticut, Wisconsin, Montana, Arizona and Alaska.

DATE:

LOCATION:

GPS COORDINATES:

NOTES:

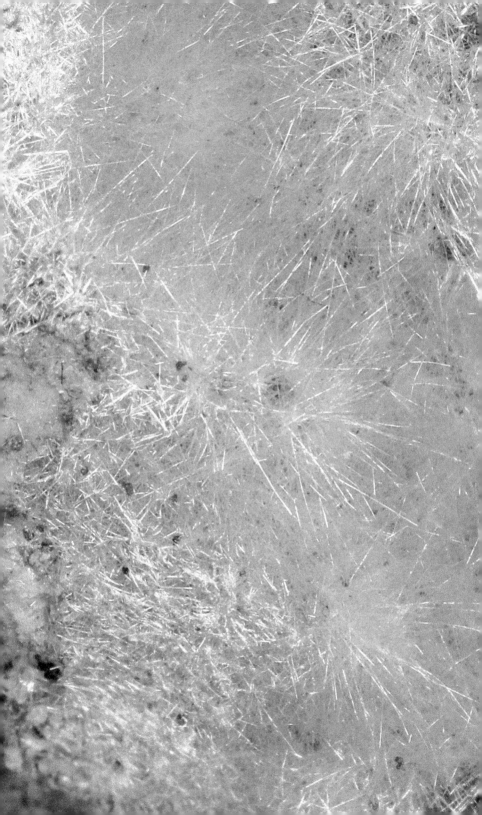

Dolomite and marcasite

Ohio is well-known for excellent specimens of crystalline dolomite, which is pictured here. These small white rhombohedrons grow on top of a thin coating of marcasite in a cavity within limestone, a rock in which both minerals very commonly occur. (Width of view: 4 m...

Chalcopyrite HARDNESS: 3.5-4 STREAK: greenish black RARITY: very common

This bright-yellow copper-bearing mineral is found all over the US, but particularly fine specimens are found in Michigan, Missouri, Kansas, Oklahoma and Colorado.

DATE:

LOCATION:

GPS COORDINATES:

NOTES:

Chlorite group HARDNESS: 2-2.5 STREAK: colorless RARITY: very common

Chlorite specimens are found in virtually every state; fine examples of this widespread group of soft, greenish minerals are found in Washington, Oregon, California, Montana, Michigan and New York.

DATE:

LOCATION:

GPS COORDINATES:

NOTES:

Chrysocolla HARDNESS: 2-4 STREAK: pale blue RARITY: common

Beautiful specimens of bright blue chrysocolla are found in California, Arizona, Utah, Michigan and Pennsylvania.

DATE:

LOCATION:

GPS COORDINATES:

NOTES:

Greenalite with hematite, limonite and jasper

Greenalite is a common constituent of banded iron formations, such as this polished specimen from Minnesota. The greenalite, yellow limonite and reddish hematite are all saturated with jasper, a form of quartz, making a hard, beautifully banded mass. (Width of view: 10 mm)

Cinnabar ⚠ **HARDNESS:** 2-2.5 **STREAK:** red **RARITY:** rare

Bright red or pink cinnabar crystals and veins are primarily found in Washington, Oregon, California, Nevada and Texas.

DATE:

LOCATION:

GPS COORDINATES:

NOTES:

Colemanite **HARDNESS:** 4-4.5 **STREAK:** white **RARITY:** rare

Glassy white colemanite crystals are found in the southwestern US, especially California and Nevada.

DATE:

LOCATION:

GPS COORDINATES:

NOTES:

Conichalcite **HARDNESS:** 4.5 **STREAK:** green **RARITY:** rare

Small, grass-green conichalcite crystals are found in the Southwest. The finest specimens come from Arizona, Utah and Nevada.

DATE:

LOCATION:

GPS COORDINATES:

NOTES:

Fluorite

Hundreds of purple intergrown cubes illustrate the classic appearance of fluorite specimens found in Illinois. Many specimens fluoresce, or glow, under ultraviolet light; in fact, the word "fluorescence" is derived from the mineral itself. (Width of view: 7 mm)

Copper HARDNESS: 2.5-3 STREAK: metallic red RARITY: common

The world's finest source of copper specimens is northern Michigan, but it is found in many other states, particularly Arizona, Colorado and Alaska.

DATE:

LOCATION:

GPS COORDINATES:

NOTES:

Corundum HARDNESS: 9 STREAK: white RARITY: uncommon

Southeastern states such as Georgia and North Carolina, and some western states, like Montana and Colorado, all produce this extremely hard mineral.

DATE:

LOCATION:

GPS COORDINATES:

NOTES:

Covellite HARDNESS: 1.5-2 STREAK: lead-gray RARITY: rare

Iridescent reddish crystals of covellite have been found all across the US. Virginia, Colorado, Wyoming, Montana, California and Alaska have all produced fine specimens.

DATE:

LOCATION:

GPS COORDINATES:

NOTES:

Aurichalcite on hemimorphite

A cluster of delicate blue aurichalcite needles stands atop a bed of glassy crystals of hemimorphite in this specimen from Arizona. The two zinc minerals often occur together and make for very attractive but fragile, specimens. (Width of view: 5 mm)

Cuprite HARDNESS: 3.5-4 STREAK: brownish red RARITY: uncommon

The best ruby-red cuprite crystals are found with copper in Arizona, New Mexico, Utah, Michigan and Pennsylvania.

DATE:

LOCATION:

GPS COORDINATES:

NOTES:

Datolite HARDNESS: 5-5.5 STREAK: colorless RARITY: uncommon

Beautiful datolite crystals come from eastern states such as Massachusetts and New Jersey and nodules (round mineral clusters) come from Michigan.

DATE:

LOCATION:

GPS COORDINATES:

NOTES:

Descloizite HARDNESS: 3-3.5 STREAK: orange to yellow RARITY: rare

Black or brown descloizite crystals come from the western states, particularly Montana, Arizona and New Mexico.

DATE:

LOCATION:

GPS COORDINATES:

NOTES:

Galena

Two tiny, three-millimeter cubes of galena grow from a sheet of limestone in this specimen from the world-famous lead mines in Oklahoma. Galena is the world's primary source of lead, and great specimens are easy to come by. (Width of view: 8 mm)

Diopside HARDNESS: 5-6 STREAK: grayish green RARITY: uncommon

Excellent crystals of this green pyroxene-group member are found in New York, Idaho, Washington and California.

DATE:

LOCATION:

GPS COORDINATES:

NOTES:

Dioptase HARDNESS: 5 STREAK: greenish blue RARITY: very rare

The United States' best specimens of dioptase's bluish-green crystals are from Arizona.

DATE:

LOCATION:

GPS COORDINATES:

NOTES:

Dolomite HARDNESS: 3.5-4 STREAK: white RARITY: very common

Dolomite is very abundant, but well-formed crystals are found in Ohio, Indiana, Michigan, Kansas and Colorado.

DATE:

LOCATION:

GPS COORDINATES:

NOTES:

Goethite

Goethite (pronounced "ger-tite") is a very common iron ore, found virtually anywhere. Most specimens are poorly formed masses or botryoidal (grape-like) crusts, unlike these well-crystallized blades from Colorado. Specimens of this quality are rare and valuable.
(Width of view: 5 mm)

Dumortierite **HARDNESS:** 7 **STREAK:** white **RARITY:** uncommon

Good specimens of this fibrous, unusually hard mineral are found in California, Arizona, New York and Maine.

DATE:

LOCATION:

GPS COORDINATES:

NOTES:

Enargite **HARDNESS:** 3 **STREAK:** grayish black **RARITY:** uncommon

Western states like Alaska, Montana, Colorado and Utah all produce this black copper-bearing mineral.

DATE:

LOCATION:

GPS COORDINATES:

NOTES:

Epidote **HARDNESS:** 6-7 **STREAK:** gray **RARITY:** very common

Epidote's characteristic yellowish-green crystals are widespread, but the best specimens come from Alaska, Washington, Idaho, Montana, Colorado and Michigan.

DATE:

LOCATION:

GPS COORDINATES:

NOTES:

Heulandite with mordenite and celadonite

In this Colorado specimen, reddish-brown heulandite and delicate tufts of white mordenite (two zeolites) sit above a thin sheet of green celadonite (a mica). Zeolites often occur together in the same specimen and can make for beautiful, and strange, collectibles.
(Width of view: 8 mm)

Fluorite HARDNESS: 4 STREAK: white RARITY: common

Fine crystalline cubes of fluorite come from Illinois, Kentucky, Tennessee, Arizona, Utah and Colorado.

DATE:

LOCATION:

GPS COORDINATES:

NOTES:

Galena ⚠ HARDNESS: 2.5 STREAK: dark gray RARITY: common

The best US specimens of this lead mineral come from Arizona, Oklahoma, Kansas and Missouri.

DATE:

LOCATION:

GPS COORDINATES:

NOTES:

Garnet group HARDNESS: 6.5-7.5 STREAK: colorless RARITY: common

Crystals from this large family of hard, metamorphic minerals are found in most states.

DATE:

LOCATION:

GPS COORDINATES:

NOTES:

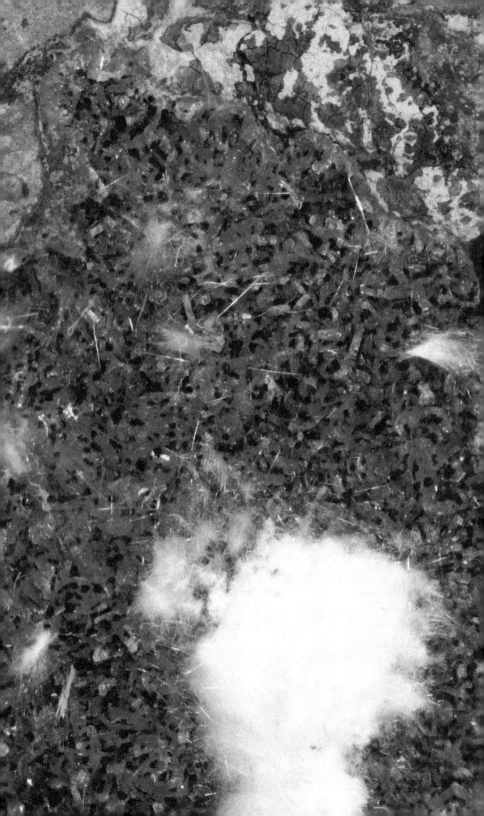

Mimetite on barite

Heavy, light-brown blades of barite are coated with orange globule of mimetite. Mimetite normally forms in small, slender, needle-like crystals, but some specimens from Arizona exhibit the less commo ball-like formations. (Width of view: 4 mm)

Garnet group *(continued)* **HARDNESS:** 6.5-7.5 **STREAK:** colorless **RARITY:** common

Fantastic specimens have come from Alaska, California, Arizona, South Dakota, Michigan, Virginia and Maine.

DATE:

LOCATION:

GPS COORDINATES:

NOTES:

Glauberite **HARDNESS:** 2.5-3 **STREAK:** white **RARITY:** uncommon

Well-formed, sharply pointed crystals of this salty mineral are found in New Jersey, Arizona and California.

DATE:

LOCATION:

GPS COORDINATES:

NOTES:

Goethite **HARDNESS:** 5-5.5 **STREAK:** yellowish-brown **RARITY:** common

This important ore of iron is found in every state, but the best specimens come from Michigan, Minnesota, Missouri and Colorado.

DATE:

LOCATION:

GPS COORDINATES:

NOTES:

Metatorbernite on uraninite

The largest crystal of metatorbernite pictured here is no more than half a millimeter across. The flat, square radioactive crystals are growing on the surface of black, botryoidal uraninite from which they are derived. Both uranium-bearing minerals are found in the southwestern states. (Width of view: 4 mm)

Gold **HARDNESS:** 2.5-3 **STREAK:** metallic yellow **RARITY:** very rare

Everyone's favorite precious metal is primarily found in Alaska, Washington, Nevada, Arizona and Colorado.

DATE:

LOCATION:

GPS COORDINATES:

NOTES:

Graphite **HARDNESS:** 1-2 **STREAK:** black **RARITY:** uncommon

New York, New Jersey, Alabama and California produce fine specimens of this soft form of carbon.

DATE:

LOCATION:

GPS COORDINATES:

NOTES:

Gypsum **HARDNESS:** 1.5-2 **STREAK:** white **RARITY:** very common

This abundant and very widespread mineral is found as fine crystals in New York, Ohio, Texas, Oklahoma, Arizona, Utah and California.

DATE:

LOCATION:

GPS COORDINATES:

NOTES:

Orthoclase with calcite, copper and chrysocolla

Orange orthoclase feldspar, green chrysocolla-coated copper and white calcite create this colorful "mess" from Michigan. Intergrowths such as this are not unusual in northern Michigan's copper mines and can make for gorgeous and interesting specimens. (Width of view: 6 mm)

Halite HARDNESS: 2-2.5 STREAK: white RARITY: common

This natural form of table salt is common in many states and is frequently found in New York, Michigan, Kansas, Utah and California.

DATE:

LOCATION:

GPS COORDINATES:

NOTES:

Hematite HARDNESS: 5-6 STREAK: brownish red RARITY: very common

Hematite, the most common form of iron ore, is found in every state, but fantastic specimens come from Minnesota, Michigan, Virginia, Colorado, Arizona and California.

DATE:

LOCATION:

GPS COORDINATES:

NOTES:

Hemimorphite HARDNESS: 4.5-5 STREAK: colorless RARITY: uncommon

Asymmetrical hemimorphite crystals primarily come from Arizona, Montana, Missouri and New Jersey.

DATE:

LOCATION:

GPS COORDINATES:

NOTES:

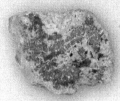

Chalcotrichite on chrysocolla

Chalcotrichite is a needle-like variety of cuprite that forms in velvet masses. This unusual specimen, from one of Arizona's many coppe mines, shows the bright red chalcotrichite growing on blue-green chrysocolla, displaying a stark contrast in colors. (Width of view: 4 mm)

Hornblende HARDNESS: 5-6 STREAK: colorless RARITY: common

Fine crystals of this dark-colored amphibole are found in New York, New Jersey, North Carolina, Arizona and California.

DATE:

LOCATION:

GPS COORDINATES:

NOTES:

Ilmenite HARDNESS: 5-6 STREAK: brownish black RARITY: common

This common constituent of gabbro is found in Massachusetts, New York, Virginia, South Carolina, Minnesota and Wyoming.

DATE:

LOCATION:

GPS COORDINATES:

NOTES:

Kaolinite HARDNESS: 2-2.5 STREAK: white RARITY: common

Masses of this soft clay mineral are widespread throughout the southern states, particularly North Carolina, Georgia, Alabama, Texas and Wyoming.

DATE:

LOCATION:

GPS COORDINATES:

NOTES:

Millerite on chalcedony

Millerite forms tiny, flexible, needle-like crystals that are normally finer than a human hair. This rare nickel mineral most frequently forms within geodes and is often the "prize" for geode-cracking collectors. This chalcedony-lined geode from Kentucky shows millerite's usual "chaotic" habit. (Width of view: 6 mm)

Kyanite HARDNESS: 4-5 lengthwise - 6-7 crosswise STREAK: colorless RARITY: uncommon

The best US specimens of blue crystals of kyanite are from the southeastern states, particularly Virginia, North Carolina, South Carolina and Georgia.

DATE:

LOCATION:

GPS COORDINATES:

NOTES:

Limonite HARDNESS: 4-5.5 STREAK: yellowish brown RARITY: very common

This mixture of iron oxide and water is found everywhere, but particularly in New York, New Jersey, Pennsylvania and Arizona.

DATE:

LOCATION:

GPS COORDINATES:

NOTES:

Magnesite HARDNESS: 3.5-4.5 STREAK: white RARITY: common

Often formed from weathered serpentine, magnesite is found in California and Arizona and other southwestern states.

DATE:

LOCATION:

GPS COORDINATES:

NOTES:

Orpiment with quartz

The unmistakable, lustrous orange-yellow crystals of orpiment are extremely soft and flexible, but easily turn to dust as they weather. Orpiment has been used as a yellow pigment for centuries, though its use is discouraged today because of orpiment's high arsenic content. (Width of view: 4 mm)

Magnetite HARDNESS: 5.5-6.5 STREAK: black RARITY: common

A magnet will stick to this widespread iron ore. Vermont, New York, New Mexico, Utah and California have produced well-crystallized specimens.

DATE:

LOCATION:

GPS COORDINATES:

NOTES:

Malachite HARDNESS: 3.5-4 STREAK: light green RARITY: uncommon

Frequently found with azurite, malachite specimens are most famous from Arizona, but also come from California and Colorado.

DATE:

LOCATION:

GPS COORDINATES:

NOTES:

Manganite HARDNESS: 3.5-4 STREAK: reddish brown to black RARITY: uncommon

Named for its manganese content, excellent manganite specimens come from Virginia, Georgia, Michigan and Arizona.

DATE:

LOCATION:

GPS COORDINATES:

NOTES:

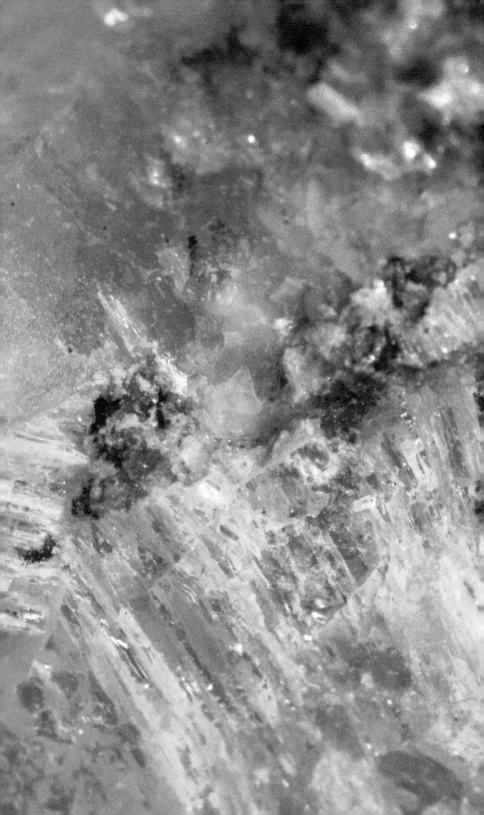

Wulfenite

Probably the most widely collected molybdenum-bearing mineral, wulfenite is one of Arizona's famous minerals. These yellow wulfenite blades are just a few millimeters in size and exhibit rounded corners. Every US mineral collector should have a specimen of Arizona wulfenite. (Width of view: 5 mm)

Marcasite **HARDNESS:** 6-6.5 **STREAK:** dark green to brown **RARITY:** common

Brassy yellow marcasite crystals are found in nearly every state, but particularly Oregon, Oklahoma, Kansas, Missouri and New York.

DATE:

LOCATION:

GPS COORDINATES:

NOTES:

Mica group **HARDNESS:** 2-2.5 **STREAK:** colorless **RARITY:** very common

Members of this large group of thin, flat, flexible minerals are found in virtually every state. Fine specimens come from Colorado, Michigan and North Carolina.

DATE:

LOCATION:

GPS COORDINATES:

NOTES:

DATE:

LOCATION:

GPS COORDINATES:

NOTES:

Diaboleite with cerussite and anglesite

Diaboleite is a very rare lead mineral found in the southwestern US. This specimen shows diaboleite's vivid blue color intermixed with gray and white swirls of massive cerussite and anglesite, two other lead minerals that are much more common. Fine crystals of diaboleite are exceedingly hard to find. (Width of view: 5 mm)

Millerite HARDNESS: 3-3.5 STREAK: greenish black RARITY: rare

Tiny, thin needles of this mineral are found in the Midwest and the Northeast, particularl in Iowa, Missouri, Wisconsin, Pennsylvania and New York.

DATE:

LOCATION:

GPS COORDINATES:

NOTES:

Mimetite HARDNESS: 3.5-4 STREAK: white RARITY: uncommon

Small orange crystals of mimetite primarily come from the southwestern states, such as Arizona, Utah and California, but also from Pennsylvania.

DATE:

LOCATION:

GPS COORDINATES:

NOTES:

Molybdenite HARDNESS: 1-1.5 STREAK: greenish to black RARITY: uncommon

Alaska, Washington, Colorado and California have all produced fine samples of this soft mineral.

DATE:

LOCATION:

GPS COORDINATES:

NOTES:

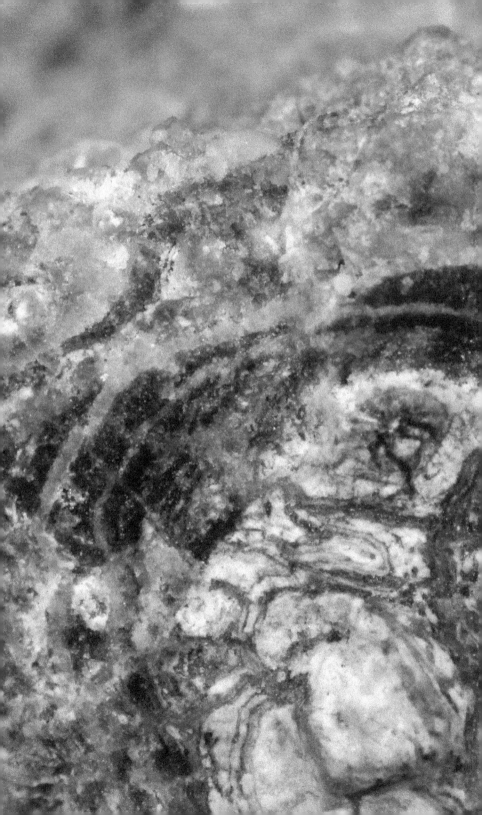

Pectolite with calcite

No state has produced better examples of pectolite than New Jersey. The white- or tan-colored fibrous crystals often occur alongside members of the zeolite mineral group, though pectolite not a zeolite itself. The specimen here is interrupted by small block of white calcite. (Width of view: 9 mm)

Monazite ☢ **HARDNESS:** 5-5.5 **STREAK:** white **RARITY:** uncommon

This often radioactive mineral is found in North Carolina, New Hampshire and Maine, among other eastern states, as well as Colorado.

DATE:

LOCATION:

GPS COORDINATES:

NOTES:

Olivine **HARDNESS:** 6.5-7 **STREAK:** colorless **RARITY:** very common

This common rock-building mineral is found everywhere, but especially in California, Arizona, Montana, Minnesota and North Carolina.

DATE:

LOCATION:

GPS COORDINATES:

NOTES:

Opal **HARDNESS:** 5.5-6.5 **STREAK:** white **RARITY:** common

This water-bearing variety of quartz is widespread throughout the West and is found in Oregon, Idaho, Utah, Nevada and Arizona.

DATE:

LOCATION:

GPS COORDINATES:

NOTES:

Purpurite with triphylite and lithiophilite

Purpurite's name derives from the Latin word for purple. This Sout
Dakota specimen illustrates how purpurite forms from the weathe
ing of green triphylite and glassy grayish-brown lithiophilite, two
lithium-bearing minerals. All three minerals are quite rare, and the
are few US collecting localities. (Width of view: 12 mm)

Orpiment ⚠ **HARDNESS:** 1.5-2 **STREAK:** lemon yellow **RARITY:** rare

Excellent crystals of this soft, orange, arsenic-bearing mineral are found in Utah, Nevada
and California.

DATE:

LOCATION:

GPS COORDINATES:

NOTES:

Orthoclase feldspar **HARDNESS:** 6-6.5 **STREAK:** white **RARITY:** very common

This very important, very common potassium-based feldspar is found everywhere, but
particularly in Arizona, Colorado and New York.

DATE:

LOCATION:

GPS COORDINATES:

NOTES:

DATE:

LOCATION:

GPS COORDINATES:

NOTES:

Pyrite

Pyrite is one of the most common collectible minerals on earth and it is easily found in any metal-bearing region. For centuries, it' brassy yellow color has fooled people into thinking they've found gold, hence the nickname "fool's gold," but pyrite is harder than gold and it has a greenish streak. (Width of view: 5 mm)

Pectolite **HARDNESS:** 4.5-5 **STREAK:** white **RARITY:** uncommon

Fibrous specimens are famous in New Jersey, but are also found in New York, Arkansas and California.

DATE:

LOCATION:

GPS COORDINATES:

NOTES:

Plagioclase feldspar group **HARDNESS:** 6 **STREAK:** white **RARITY:** common

This extremely common and important feldspar group is a constituent of many rocks. Fine examples come from Georgia, Minnesota, Montana and Colorado.

DATE:

LOCATION:

GPS COORDINATES:

NOTES:

DATE:

LOCATION:

GPS COORDINATES:

NOTES:

Realgar in quartz

Arsenic-bearing realgar is highly collectible for its unmistakable blood-red color, seen occurring with quartz in this specimen from Nevada. Realgar's crystals are light-sensitive and will darken if not kept in a dark storage container. (Width of view: 9 mm)

Prehnite HARDNESS: 6-6.5 STREAK: colorless RARITY: common

Michigan, Virginia, New Jersey and Connecticut all produce fine specimens of this light-green mineral.

DATE:

LOCATION:

GPS COORDINATES:

NOTES:

Psilomelane HARDNESS: 5-6 STREAK: black RARITY: common

Botryoidal (grape-like) crusts of this manganese mineral group come from many states, but particularly Arizona, Utah, Colorado, Montana and Virginia.

DATE:

LOCATION:

GPS COORDINATES:

NOTES:

Pumpellyite group HARDNESS: 6 STREAK: white RARITY: rare

The Keweenaw Peninsula in Michigan produces the finest specimens of pumpellyite, though it is also found in California.

DATE:

LOCATION:

GPS COORDINATES:

NOTES:

Agate with copper

There are several theories as to how they form, but the copper-banded agates of the Keweenaw Peninsula in northern Michigan are truly one-of-a-kind specimens. Also called "copper replacement agates," these gems form no larger than an inch or two, but still command very high prices. (Width of view: 6 mm)

Pyrite HARDNESS: 6-6.5 STREAK: greenish black RARITY: very common

This iron mineral is found in virtually every state, especially Colorado, Arkansas, Illinois and Pennsylvania.

DATE:

LOCATION:

GPS COORDINATES:

NOTES:

Pyrolusite HARDNESS: 6-6.5 STREAK: bluish black RARITY: uncommon

Well-formed, fan-shaped crystal groupings of this widespread manganese mineral come from Michigan, Minnesota, Utah and Arizona.

DATE:

LOCATION:

GPS COORDINATES:

NOTES:

Pyromorphite HARDNESS: 3.5-4 STREAK: pale yellow RARITY: uncommon

Pennsylvania, Virginia, North Carolina, Arizona and Idaho are home to fine specimens of this lead-based mineral.

DATE:

LOCATION:

GPS COORDINATES:

NOTES:

Copper on prehnite and calcite

Many newer collectors don't realize that native metals can occur naturally in wire form. This specimen of Michigan copper shows the peculiar wire habit, formed in a cavity filled with prehnite, calcite and very small crystals of epidote and datolite. (Width of view: 5 mm - Specimen courtesy of John Perona)

Pyrophyllite **HARDNESS:** 1-2 **STREAK:** white **RARITY:** uncommon

This soft mineral is difficult to distinguish from talc. Great specimens are found in California, Utah, North Carolina and Georgia.

DATE:

LOCATION:

GPS COORDINATES:

NOTES:

Pyrrhotite **HARDNESS:** 3.5-4.5 **STREAK:** dark gray **RARITY:** uncommon

Maine, Connecticut, Tennessee, Washington, Idaho and California produce the best examples of this unique metallic mineral.

DATE:

LOCATION:

GPS COORDINATES:

NOTES:

Quartz **HARDNESS:** 7 **STREAK:** white **RARITY:** very common

As the single most abundant mineral on earth, fine quartz specimens are found anywhere

DATE:

LOCATION:

GPS COORDINATES:

NOTES:

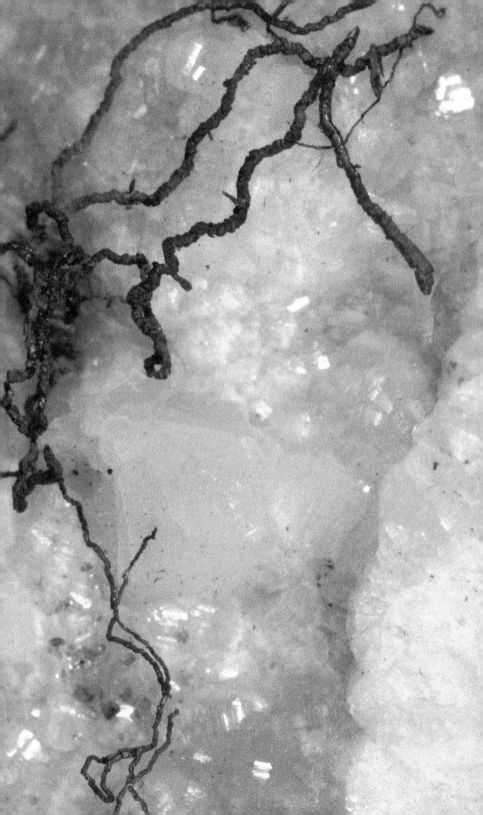

Rhodochrosite

Closely related to siderite, dolomite and calcite, rhodochrosite is an extremely collectible mineral found in many states. Colorado has become famous as one of the world's best sites for rhodochrosite crystals, but this specimen from Michigan shows the prized, intense rose color. (Width of view: 9 mm)

Quartz *(continued)* **HARDNESS:** 7 **STREAK:** white **RARITY:** very common

Amethyst (purple quartz) is found in Minnesota and South Carolina. Gray smoky quartz is found in Colorado and Montana. Fine clear crystal points are found in Pennsylvania, Arkansas and Idaho.

DATE:

LOCATION:

GPS COORDINATES:

NOTES:

DATE:

LOCATION:

GPS COORDINATES:

NOTES:

Realgar ⚠ **HARDNESS:** 1.5-2 **STREAK:** orange-yellow **RARITY:** uncommon

Beautiful, well-formed red crystals of arsenic-rich realgar come from Washington, Utah, Nevada and California.

DATE:

LOCATION:

GPS COORDINATES:

NOTES:

Rosasite on limonite

Rosasite is an uncommon copper- and zinc-bearing mineral found in southwestern states. Seen here in its classic "puff ball" structure these round crystal groupings are about 2 millimeters wide at their largest, growing in a cavity within a mass of limonite. (Width of view: 10 mm)

Rhodonite HARDNESS: 5.5-6 STREAK: colorless RARITY: uncommon

This red manganese mineral is found as fine crystals in New Jersey, Massachusetts and Colorado.

DATE:

LOCATION:

GPS COORDINATES:

NOTES:

Rhodochrosite HARDNESS: 3.5-4 STREAK: white RARITY: common

Some of the world's finest crystals of this widespread pink mineral are from California, Colorado, Montana and Michigan.

DATE:

LOCATION:

GPS COORDINATES:

NOTES:

Rutile HARDNESS: 6-6.5 STREAK: white RARITY: common

This common titanium mineral is found in most states, particularly California, Pennsylvania Connecticut, South Carolina and Georgia.

DATE:

LOCATION:

GPS COORDINATES:

NOTES:

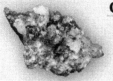

Calcite with copper and chlorite inclusions

What's making this colorless calcite look orange? Native copper crystals are encased within it—a very rare combination from northern Michigan. Below it is a thin crust of green calcite, colored by the chlorite contained within. (Width of view: 8 mm)

Scheelite **HARDNESS:** 4.5-5 **STREAK:** white to yellow **RARITY:** rare

Scheelite is a rare tungsten mineral found as fine crystals in Colorado, Arizona, Utah, California and Alaska.

DATE:

LOCATION:

GPS COORDINATES:

NOTES:

Serpentine group **HARDNESS:** 3-5 **STREAK:** white **RARITY:** very common

This group of green, greasy-feeling minerals is found in most states, especially California, Arizona, New York and New Jersey.

DATE:

LOCATION:

GPS COORDINATES:

NOTES:

Siderite **HARDNESS:** 3.5-4 **STREAK:** white **RARITY:** common

Siderite is a common iron-based cousin of calcite, and it is found in Connecticut, Pennsylvania, Minnesota, Colorado, Idaho and many other states.

DATE:

LOCATION:

GPS COORDINATES:

NOTES:

Magnetite

Crystals of this mineral jut from the surface of white dolomite and quartz. Its name derives from its most easily identified characteristic: magnetite attracts a magnet. It is much more common than many people know and is easily found as grains on dark sand beaches. (Width of view: 8 mm)

Silver HARDNESS: 2.5-3 STREAK: metallic gray RARITY: rare

Michigan's Keweenaw Peninsula is one of the finest localities, as well as Colorado, Arizona and California.

DATE:

LOCATION:

GPS COORDINATES:

NOTES:

Skutterudite series HARDNESS: 5.5-6 STREAK: gray RARITY: rare

This small group of metallic minerals is found in small amounts across the US, particularly in California, New Mexico, Colorado and New Jersey.

DATE:

LOCATION:

GPS COORDINATES:

NOTES:

Smithsonite HARDNESS: 4-4.5 STREAK: white RARITY: uncommon

Pennsylvania, Kentucky, Arkansas, Idaho and Utah are well-known sources of this zinc mineral.

DATE:

LOCATION:

GPS COORDINATES:

NOTES:

Siderite with pyrite

This specimen of siderite from Colorado shows its classic bladed habit and creamy-brown color. As an iron mineral, it is commonly found in mining regions alongside other iron-bearing minerals, such as the brassy pyrites shown here. (Width of view: 8 mm)

Sphalerite HARDNESS: 3.5-4 STREAK: light brown RARITY: common

New Jersey, Tennessee, Missouri, Oklahoma and Colorado have produced amazing specimens of sphalerite.

DATE:

LOCATION:

GPS COORDINATES:

NOTES:

Spinel HARDNESS: 7.5-8 STREAK: white RARITY: rare

Very fine crystals of this semi-precious mineral have been found in California, Colorado, North Carolina, New Jersey and New York.

DATE:

LOCATION:

GPS COORDINATES:

NOTES:

Staurolite HARDNESS: 7-7.5 STREAK: white RARITY: uncommon

Staurolite is widespread in schists across the US, but particularly in New Mexico, New Hampshire, Georgia, North Carolina and South Carolina.

DATE:

LOCATION:

GPS COORDINATES:

NOTES:

Thomsonite

Thomsonite is an uncommon zeolite that normally forms in delicate white sprays of needle-like crystals. On Minnesota's Lake Superior shores, however, it forms compact nodules in basalt. Since the depletion of Scotland's similar thomsonite nodules, Minnesota and Michigan are the only places to find them. (Width of view: 12 mm)

Stibnite HARDNESS: 2 STREAK: dark gray RARITY: uncommon

The country's best samples of stibnite's long, slender, silver-colored crystals are found in Oregon, California, Idaho, Utah and Nevada.

DATE:

LOCATION:

GPS COORDINATES:

NOTES:

Sulfur HARDNESS: 1.5-2.5 STREAK: white RARITY: rare

California, Utah, Texas, Michigan and Connecticut produce finely formed, bright yellow crystals of this rare native element.

DATE:

LOCATION:

GPS COORDINATES:

NOTES:

Talc HARDNESS: 1 STREAK: white RARITY: common

This incredibly soft, green mineral is widespread throughout the US, but fine crystallized specimens come from Washington, Utah, Michigan, Connecticut, Vermont and New Jersey.

DATE:

LOCATION:

GPS COORDINATES:

NOTES:

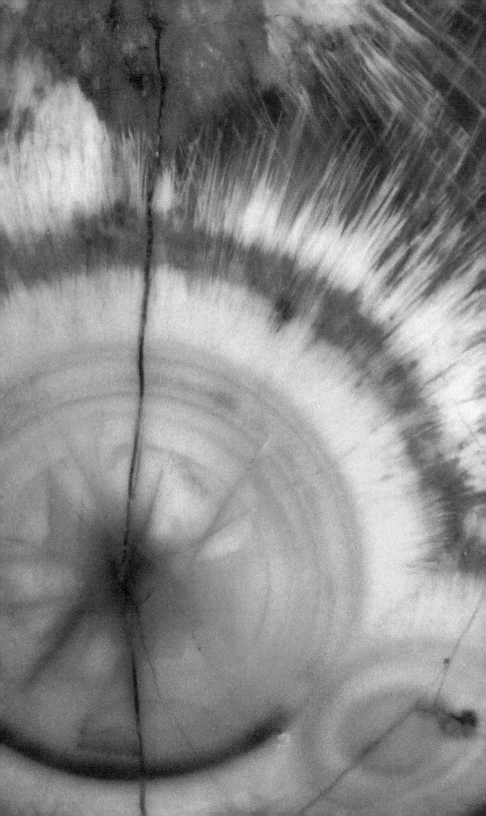

Jasper

Jasper is a microscopically grained variety of quartz that can occur in any color. A polished sample of "Biggs jasper," a particular variety from Oregon, is pictured here. It formed when layers of clay and volcanic ash were saturated with water containing silica (quartz material). (Width of view: 7 mm)

Tetrahedrite HARDNESS: 3-4 STREAK: black RARITY: uncommon

Named for its classic tetrahedral crystals, tetrahedrite is found in Idaho, Utah, Colorado and other western states.

DATE:

LOCATION:

GPS COORDINATES:

NOTES:

Titanite HARDNESS: 5-5.5 STREAK: white RARITY: uncommon

Also called "sphene," fine crystals of this titanium-bearing mineral come from California, Colorado, Montana and New York.

DATE:

LOCATION:

GPS COORDINATES:

NOTES:

Topaz HARDNESS: 8 STREAK: colorless RARITY: uncommon

New Hampshire, North Carolina and Colorado produce topaz, but the finest specimens come from Utah.

DATE:

LOCATION:

GPS COORDINATES:

NOTES:

"Tiffany stone"

"Tiffany stone," also known as "opalized fluorite," is a strange combination of minerals found only in Utah. It results from volcanic gasses and contains fluorite, opal, chalcedony, beryl, bertrandite, quartz and manganese. The original collecting site is closed and specimens are quite valuable. (Width of view: 4 mm)

Tourmaline group **HARDNESS:** 7-7.5 **STREAK:** white **RARITY:** uncommon

The best specimens of these long, slender, grooved crystals are found in California, South Dakota, Michigan and Maine.

DATE:

LOCATION:

GPS COORDINATES:

NOTES:

Tremolite ⚠ **HARDNESS:** 5-6 **STREAK:** colorless **RARITY:** common

This common member of the amphibole group is found in many states, particularly in the East, including New York, Connecticut and South Carolina. It is also abundant in the West where it is found in Arizona and California.

DATE:

LOCATION:

GPS COORDINATES:

NOTES:

Turquoise **HARDNESS:** 5-6 **STREAK:** white to pale green **RARITY:** uncommon

Gem-grade masses come from Nevada, Utah and Arizona, but tiny crystals occur in Virginia.

DATE:

LOCATION:

GPS COORDINATES:

NOTES:

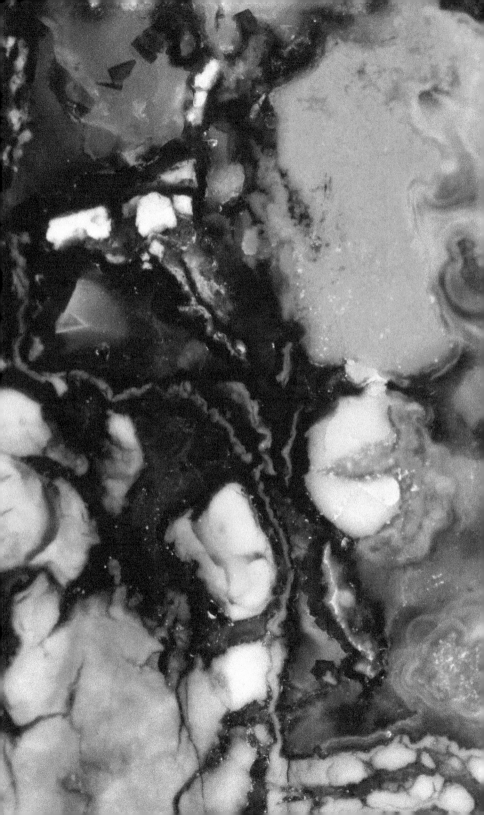

Vanadinite with wulfenite

Tiny, red, six-sided vanadinite crystals lie in no particular order atop a bed of even tinier brown wulfenite crystals. The two lead-bearing minerals form bright, lustrous crystals that are extremely popular with Arizona's collectors. (Width of view: 16 mm)

Uraninite ☢ HARDNESS: 5-6 STREAK: brownish black RARITY: uncommon

Finely crystallized black cubes of this radioactive mineral can be found in Colorado, Arizona, Maine and Connecticut.

DATE:

LOCATION:

GPS COORDINATES:

NOTES:

Vanadinite HARDNESS: 3 STREAK: white to yellow RARITY: uncommon

The southwestern states, particularly New Mexico, Arizona and California, produce this beautiful, brightly colored mineral.

DATE:

LOCATION:

GPS COORDINATES:

NOTES:

Variscite HARDNESS: 4-4.5 STREAK: white RARITY: uncommon

Arkansas produces some of this country's best variscite, but Utah has it as well.

DATE:

LOCATION:

GPS COORDINATES:

NOTES:

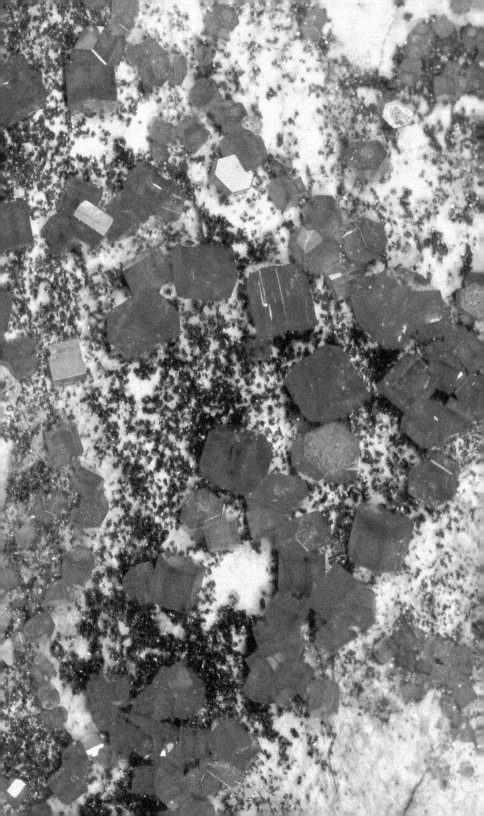

Chalcopyrite with aragonite

These curious, pyramid-shaped aggregates of chalcopyrite crystals formed beside a crust of hard, white aragonite in this Michigan specimen. Combinations like this are some of the most interesting samples you can add to your collection. (Width of view: 8 mm)

Vesuvianite HARDNESS: 6.5 STREAK: white RARITY: rare

Also known as idocrase, vesuvianite is rare in the US, but it occurs in California, Colorado, Montana and New Jersey.

DATE:

LOCATION:

GPS COORDINATES:

NOTES:

Wavellite HARDNESS: 3.5-4 STREAK: white RARITY: uncommon

Some of the world's finest wavellites come from Arkansas, but it is also found in Pennsylvania and Virginia.

DATE:

LOCATION:

GPS COORDINATES:

NOTES:

Willemite HARDNESS: 5.5 STREAK: white RARITY: uncommon

Willemite is found in Arizona, but nowhere else in the world produces willemite with brighter fluorescence than New Jersey.

DATE:

LOCATION:

GPS COORDINATES:

NOTES:

Variscite

Several places around the US produce variscite, an attractive green collectible. The specimen here is from Arkansas, where it commonly forms as coatings within cracks in rock. Oddly, variscite does not get its green color from copper or nickel, the usual suspects for green coloration, but rather from aluminum. (Width of view: 10 mm)

Wolframite HARDNESS: 4-4.5 STREAK: brown to black RARITY: rare

This small group of tungsten-based minerals is found in few places, but fine crystals come from Nevada, Colorado and North Carolina.

DATE:

LOCATION:

GPS COORDINATES:

NOTES:

Wulfenite HARDNESS: 3 STREAK: white RARITY: uncommon

The best wulfenites come from various mines in Arizona, specifically the Red Cloud Mine.

DATE:

LOCATION:

GPS COORDINATES:

NOTES:

Zeolite group HARDNESS: 3.5-4 STREAK: colorless RARITY: common

This huge group of water-bearing minerals commonly forms in cavities within basalt.

DATE:

LOCATION:

GPS COORDINATES:

NOTES:

Thomsonite

Oregon is well-known for its zeolites, including the gray thomson pictured here. This very rare and strange formation of thomsonite "worms" nearly defies description. Thomsonite more commonly forms as sprays of needle-like crystals. (Width of view: 7 mm)

Zeolite group *(continued)* HARDNESS: 3.5-4 STREAK: colorless RARITY: common

Zeolites are common and widespread, but Washington, Oregon, Arizona, Colorado, Minnesota, Michigan and New Jersey all produce fine zeolites.

DATE:

LOCATION:

GPS COORDINATES:

NOTES:

Zincite HARDNESS: 4 STREAK: orange-yellow RARITY: very rare

The finest US specimens of this rare ore of zinc come from New Jersey.

DATE:

LOCATION:

GPS COORDINATES:

NOTES:

Zircon HARDNESS: 7.5 STREAK: colorless RARITY: rare

New Jersey, North Carolina, South Dakota, Oklahoma, Idaho and Colorado produce very fine zircon crystals.

DATE:

LOCATION:

GPS COORDINATES:

NOTES:

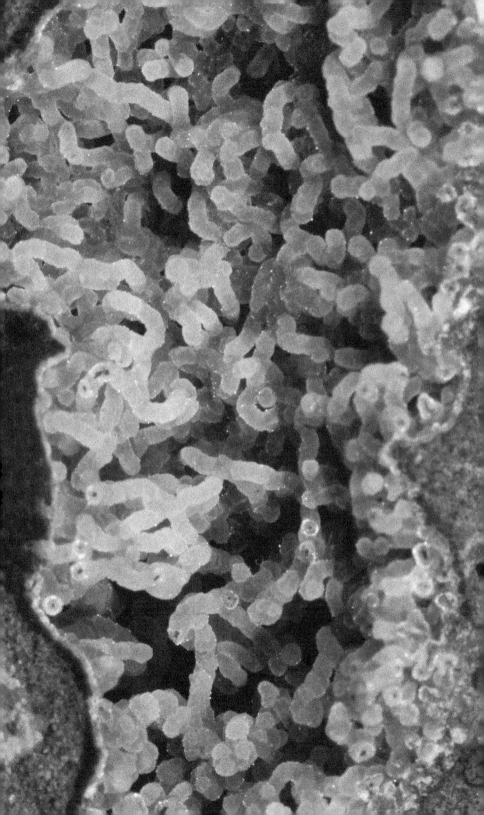

Wulfenite

Pictured here are two flat, square wulfenite crystals from the Red Cloud Mine in southwestern Arizona. This locality is world-famous for its bright orange-red wulfenite crystals, colored by trace amounts of the element chromium. Specimens from the mine were once abundant but are now much rarer. (Width of view: 5 mm)

Notes

Here you can write or draw anything from your mineral collecting adventures. Good examples of things to take note of are geological observations from your travels, detailed descriptions of unique mineral occurrences, directions to particular rock outcroppings and GPS coordinates of collecting sites. Or, you could treat these pages as a place to write your own "field guide," with notes on how to find your favorite collecting site as well as which tools you'll need and tips on how to work the area.

Wavellite

Arkansas produces some of the finest wavellite specimens in the world, including the one shown here. The famous radial appearance of wavellite is actually the mineral's cross-section, only seen i broken specimens. An intact specimen of wavellite forms as a gree rounded ball. (Width of view: 12 mm)

Notes

Quartz

Standing tall off of a cluster of quartz crystals is a scepter, an unusual and rare formation of quartz. Scepters can grow to any size and some are quite large, but this one from Arizona is a mere three millimeters long. (Width of view: 6 mm)

Notes

Notes

Notes

Notes

Notes

Checklist

As you can imagine, the United States has many more than the 116 minerals featured in th book. As your collection grows, you'll likely find or buy a rare mineral not found in the log portion of this book. And you'll probably pick up a few rocks here and there and want to record what you have. This checklist catalogs 332 of the nation's minerals, rocks and fossils It includes all the minerals from the log as well as significant individual members of the major mineral groups, such as the zeolite group and serpentine group. It also includes 166 additional uncommon minerals to keep you collecting for years.

Without question, there are some minerals with which every collector must be well-acquainted. Everything about these essential minerals, including their appearance, hardnes composition and crystal structure, is important to understanding not only the mineral itself but all similar and related minerals. Within this list are 55 minerals, marked with an asterisk (*), that amateur collectors should focus on finding, studying and understanding before hunting for anything else. And the more specimens of each mineral you collect, the better you'll be at recognizing that mineral—calcite, for example, has been recorded to have over 800 crystal habits, so collecting as many varied specimens as possible would be wise. If the radioactivity symbol (☢) is next to a mineral it means that it contains either uranium or thorium and is radioactive. If an exclamation point (⚠) is next to a mineral, it is potentially hazardous.

Rocks are generally considered to be less collectible; however, being able to tell one type of rock from another, even in just a general sense, is extremely important to collectors. Listed here are 30 important and collectible rock types found in all corners of the United States th every rock hound should be able to identify with some practice. Finally, there is a short list of fossils that collectors should consider seeking out. Fossils can be found in every state and many kinds are available to the amateur, but very common and collectible species or fossils groups are listed here.

MINERALS

☐ Acanthite	☐ Andalusite *	☐ Aragonite *
☐ Acmite (Aegirine)	☐ Andesine	☐ Arsenic ⚠
☐ Actinolite	☐ Andradite	☐ Arsenopyrite
☐ Adamite	☐ Anglesite ⚠	☐ Astrophyllite
☐ Albite	☐ Anhydrite	☐ Atacamite
☐ Algodonite	☐ Annabergite	☐ Augite *
☐ Allanite	☐ Anorthite	☐ Aurichalcite
☐ Almandine	☐ Anthophyllite	☐ Austinite
☐ Alunite	☐ Antigorite	☐ Autunite ☢
☐ Amblygonite	☐ Antimony	☐ Axinite
☐ Analcime	☐ Apatite *	☐ Azurite *
☐ Anatase	☐ Apophyllite	☐ Babingtonite

- [ ] Barite ✶
- [ ] Bauxite
- [ ] Benitoite
- [ ] Bertrandite
- [ ] Beryl ✶
- [ ] Beryllonite
- [ ] Biotite
- [ ] Bismuth
- [ ] Bismuthinite
- [ ] Bixbyite
- [ ] Boleite
- [ ] Borax
- [ ] Bornite
- [ ] Boulangerite
- [ ] Bournonite
- [ ] Brochantite
- [ ] Brookite
- [ ] Brucite
- [ ] Bytownite
- [ ] Calaverite
- [ ] Calcite ✶
- [ ] Caledonite
- [ ] Carnotite ☢
- [ ] Cassiterite
- [ ] Celestine ✶
- [ ] Cerussite ⚠ ✶
- [ ] Chabazite
- [ ] Chalcanthite ⚠
- [ ] Chalcedony ✶
- [ ] Chalcocite
- [ ] Chalcopyrite ✶
- [ ] Chamosite
- [ ] Childrenite

- [ ] Chlorargyrite
- [ ] Chlorite group ✶
- [ ] Chondrodite
- [ ] Chromite
- [ ] Chrysoberyl
- [ ] Chrysocolla ✶
- [ ] Chrysotile ⚠
- [ ] Cinnabar ⚠
- [ ] Clinochlore
- [ ] Clinozoisite
- [ ] Cobaltite
- [ ] Colemanite
- [ ] Columbite
- [ ] Conichalcite
- [ ] Copiapite
- [ ] Copper ✶
- [ ] Cordierite
- [ ] Corundum ✶
- [ ] Covellite
- [ ] Crocoite
- [ ] Cryolite
- [ ] Cuprite ✶
- [ ] Cyanotrichite
- [ ] Danburite
- [ ] Datolite
- [ ] Descloizite
- [ ] Diaboleite
- [ ] Diamond
- [ ] Diaspore
- [ ] Diopside ✶
- [ ] Dioptase
- [ ] Dolomite ✶
- [ ] Domeykite

- [ ] Dravite
- [ ] Dufrénite
- [ ] Dumortierite
- [ ] Elbaite
- [ ] Enargite
- [ ] Enstatite
- [ ] Epidote ✶
- [ ] Epsomite
- [ ] Erythrite
- [ ] Eudialyte
- [ ] Fayalite
- [ ] Fluorite ✶
- [ ] Forsterite
- [ ] Franklinite
- [ ] Galena ⚠ ✶
- [ ] Garnet group ✶
- [ ] Glauberite
- [ ] Glaucophane
- [ ] Goethite ✶
- [ ] Gold ✶
- [ ] Graphite
- [ ] Greenockite
- [ ] Grossular
- [ ] Grunerite
- [ ] Gypsum ✶
- [ ] Halite ✶
- [ ] Hedenbergite
- [ ] Hematite ✶
- [ ] Hemimorphite
- [ ] Herderite
- [ ] Heulandite
- [ ] Hornblende ✶
- [ ] Howlite

- ☐ Humite group
- ☐ Hureaulite
- ☐ Hydrozincite
- ☐ Hypersthene
- ☐ Ilmenite *
- ☐ Inesite
- ☐ Jadeite
- ☐ Jamesonite
- ☐ Jarosite
- ☐ Kaolinite *
- ☐ Kernite
- ☐ Kyanite
- ☐ Labradorite
- ☐ Lawsonite
- ☐ Lazulite
- ☐ Lazurite
- ☐ Leadhillite
- ☐ Lepidolite
- ☐ Leucite
- ☐ Libethenite
- ☐ Limonite *
- ☐ Linarite
- ☐ Lithiophilite
- ☐ Lizardite
- ☐ Löllingite ⚠
- ☐ Magnesite *
- ☐ Magnetite *
- ☐ Malachite *
- ☐ Manganite
- ☐ Marcasite *
- ☐ Margarite
- ☐ Massicot ⚠
- ☐ Melanterite ⚠

- ☐ Mercury ⚠
- ☐ Mesolite
- ☐ Miargyrite
- ☐ Mica group *
- ☐ Microcline
- ☐ Microlite
- ☐ Millerite
- ☐ Mimetite
- ☐ Molybdenite
- ☐ Monazite ☢
- ☐ Montmorillonite
- ☐ Muscovite
- ☐ Natrolite
- ☐ Nepheline
- ☐ Neptunite
- ☐ Niccolite
- ☐ Nickeline
- ☐ Niter
- ☐ Oligoclase
- ☐ Olivenite
- ☐ Olivine *
- ☐ Opal *
- ☐ Orpiment ⚠
- ☐ Orthoclase *
- ☐ Pargasite
- ☐ Pectolite
- ☐ Pentlandite
- ☐ Petzite
- ☐ Phenakite
- ☐ Phlogopite
- ☐ Phosgenite
- ☐ Phosphuranylite ☢
- ☐ Plagioclase *

- ☐ Platinum
- ☐ Polybasite
- ☐ Powellite
- ☐ Prehnite
- ☐ Proustite
- ☐ Psilomelane
- ☐ Pumpellyite
- ☐ Purpurite
- ☐ Pyrargyrite
- ☐ Pyrite *
- ☐ Pyrochlore
- ☐ Pyrolusite
- ☐ Pyromorphite
- ☐ Pyrope
- ☐ Pyrophyllite
- ☐ Pyrrhotite
- ☐ Quartz *
- ☐ Realgar ⚠
- ☐ Rhodonite
- ☐ Rhodochrosite *
- ☐ Riebeckite
- ☐ Rosasite
- ☐ Rutile *
- ☐ Samarskite ☢
- ☐ Scapolite series
- ☐ Scheelite
- ☐ Schorl
- ☐ Scolecite
- ☐ Scorodite
- ☐ Serpentine group *
- ☐ Shattuckite
- ☐ Siderite *
- ☐ Sillimanite

- [ ] Silver *
- [ ] Skutterudite
- [ ] Smithsonite
- [ ] Sodalite
- [ ] Spessartine
- [ ] Sphalerite *
- [ ] Spinel group
- [ ] Spodumene
- [ ] Staurolite *
- [ ] Stephanite
- [ ] Stibnite
- [ ] Stilbite
- [ ] Strontianite
- [ ] Sulfur *
- [ ] Sylvanite
- [ ] Sylvite

- [ ] Talc *
- [ ] Tantalite
- [ ] Tellurium
- [ ] Tephroite
- [ ] Tetrahedrite
- [ ] Thenardite
- [ ] Thomsonite
- [ ] Thorite ☢
- [ ] Titanite (Sphene)
- [ ] Topaz
- [ ] Torbernite ☢
- [ ] Tourmaline group *
- [ ] Tremolite ⚠ *
- [ ] Triphylite
- [ ] Turquoise
- [ ] Ulexite

- [ ] Uraninite ☢
- [ ] Uranophane ☢
- [ ] Vanadinite
- [ ] Variscite
- [ ] Vesuvianite
- [ ] Vivianite
- [ ] Wardite
- [ ] Wavellite
- [ ] Witherite
- [ ] Wolframite series
- [ ] Wollastonite
- [ ] Wulfenite
- [ ] Zeolite group *
- [ ] Zincite
- [ ] Zircon
- [ ] Zoisite

OCKS

- [ ] Andesite
- [ ] Basalt
- [ ] Breccia
- [ ] Chert
- [ ] Coal
- [ ] Conglomerate
- [ ] Dacite
- [ ] Diabase
- [ ] Diorite
- [ ] Gabbro

- [ ] Gneiss
- [ ] Granite
- [ ] Granodiorite
- [ ] Hornfels
- [ ] Kimberlite
- [ ] Marble
- [ ] Mudstone
- [ ] Pegmatite
- [ ] Peridotite
- [ ] Quartzite

- [ ] Rhyolite
- [ ] Sandstone
- [ ] Schist
- [ ] Serpentinite
- [ ] Shale
- [ ] Siltstone
- [ ] Skarn
- [ ] Syenite
- [ ] Tuff
- [ ] Unakite

FOSSILS

- [ ] Ammonite
- [ ] Baculites
- [ ] Bone
- [ ] Brachiopod
- [ ] Coprolite
- [ ] Crinoid
- [ ] Dinosaur tooth
- [ ] Fern
- [ ] Fish

- [ ] Fossil nodule
- [ ] Horn coral
- [ ] Leaf
- [ ] Orthoceras
- [ ] Petoskey Stone
- [ ] Petrified wood
- [ ] Reed
- [ ] Shark tooth
- [ ] Snail shell

- [ ] Stromatolite
- [ ] Trilobite

ACCESSORY MINERAL: A mineral not important to the identification of a rock, e.g., minerals that formed later within cavities in the rock

AGGREGATE: An accumulation or mass of crystals

ALTERATION: Chemical changes within a rock or mineral due to the addition of mineral solutions

AMPHIBOLE: A large group of important rock-forming minerals, commonly with a fibrous appearance

AMYGDULE: A vesicle, or gas bubble, that has been filled with a secondary mineral

ASSOCIATED: Minerals that often occur together due to similar chemical traits

ASBESTOS: A very fibrous, flexible, silky-feeling mineral formation; it can refer to several different minerals, especially chrysotile serpentine and tremolite

BAND: An easily identified layer within a rock or mineral

BED: A large, flat mass of rock, generally sedimentary

BOTRYOIDAL: Crusts of a mineral formed in rounded masses, resembling a bunch of grapes

BRECCIA: A coarse-grained rock composed of broken, angular rock fragments that have been solidified together

CHALCEDONY: A massive, microcrystalline variety of quartz with a waxy luster

CLAY: Extremely fine-grained sediment consisting primarily of clay minerals

CLAY MINERALS: A loosely defined group of aluminum-rich minerals that occur as microscopic crystals, including montmorillonite, kaolinite, illite and smectite

CLEAVAGE: The property of a mineral to break along the planes of its crystal structure, which reflects its internal crystal shape

COMPACT: Dense, tightly formed rocks or minerals

CONCENTRIC: Circular, ringed banding, resembling a bull's-eye pattern, with larger rings encompassing smaller rings

CONCRETION: A hard, generally rounded shape resulting from sediment accumulating around a central nucleus, particularly fossil material

CONCHOIDAL FRACTURE: The property of a mineral to produce rounded, half-moon-shaped cracks when struck

CONTACT METAMORPHISM: Rock metamorphosis taking place as a result of magma being forced into a body of pre-existing rock

CRYPTOCRYSTALLINE: Crystal structure too small to be seen, even by a conventional microscope

CRYSTAL: A solid body with a repeating atomic structure formed by the hardening of an element or chemical compound

CUBIC: A box-like structure with six equal sides

DEHYDRATE: To lose water contained within

DENDRITE: A mineral structure resembling the formation of a tree and its branches

DRUSE: A coating of small crystals on the surface of another rock or mineral. Also spelled "druze"

DRUSY: Referring to a formation of druse, e.g., "drusy quartz." Also spelled "druzy"

DULL: A mineral that is poorly reflective

EARTHY: Resembling soil; a mineral with dull luster and rough texture

EFFERVESCE: When a mineral placed in an acid gives off bubbles caused by the mineral dissolving

EFFLORESCENCE: A mineral powder or coating produced on the surface of rocks via the evaporation of mineral-bearing water

FELDSPAR: An extremely common and diverse group of light-colored minerals that are most prevalent within rocks and make up the majority of the earth's crust

FIBROUS: Fine, rod-like crystals that resemble cloth fibers

FLOAT: Metal that has been scraped up, moved and rounded by glaciers, resulting in a "nugget"

FLUORESCENCE: The property of a mineral to give off visible light when exposed to ultraviolet light radiation

FRACTURE: The way a mineral breaks or cracks when struck, often referred to in terms of shape or texture

GEODE: A round, hollow rock formation often containing a drusy coating of crystals within, especially quartz

GLASSY: A mineral with a reflectivity similar to window glass, also known as "vitreous luster"

GNEISS: A rock that has been metamorphosed so that some of its minerals are aligned in parallel bands

GRANITIC: Pertaining to granite or granite-like rocks

GRANULAR: A texture or appearance of rocks or minerals that consist of grains or particles

GROUP: Minerals with similar chemical compounds and crystal structures

HEXAGONAL: A six-sided structure

HOST: A rock or mineral on or in which other rocks and minerals occur

HYDROUS: Containing water

IGNEOUS ROCK: Rock resulting from the cooling and solidification of molten rock such as magma or lava

IMPURITY: A foreign mineral within a host mineral that often changes properties of the host, particularly color

INCLUSION: A mineral that is encased or impressed within a host mineral

IRIDESCENCE: When a mineral exhibits a rainbow-like play of color

LAMELLAR: Minerals composed of thin parallel crystals arranged into book- or gill-like aggregates

LAVA: Molten rock that has reached the earth's surface

LIME: Calcium oxide, a chemical compound containing calcium and oxygen. Generally describes calcium-rich compounds or minerals

LODESTONE: A naturally charged variety of the mineral magnetite. It acts as a natural magnet and will attract iron

LUSTER: The way in which a mineral reflects light off of its surface, described by its intensity

MAGMA: Molten rock that remains deep within the earth

MAGNETISM: The ability of an iron-rich rock to attract a magnet

MASSIVE: Minerals that don't occur in individual crystals but rather as a solid, compact concentration; rocks can also be described as massive. In geology, "massive" is rarely used in reference to size

MATRIX: The rock in which a mineral forms

METAMORPHIC ROCK: Rock that formed after existing igneous or sedimentary rocks were altered due to heat and pressure

METAMORPHOSED: A rock or mineral that has already undergone metamorphosis

MICA: A large group of minerals that occur as thin flakes arranged into layered aggregates resembling a book

MICACEOUS: Mica-like in nature; a mineral aggregate consisting of thin sheets

MICROCRYSTALLINE: Crystal structure too small to see with the naked eye, requiring the use of a microscope

MINERAL: A naturally occurring chemical compound or native element that solidifies with a definite internal crystal structure

NATIVE ELEMENT: An element found naturally free of any other elements, e.g., copper

NODULE: A rounded mass consisting of a mineral, generally formed within a vesicle

OCTAGONAL: An eight-sided structure

OCTAHEDRON: A structure with eight-faces, resembling two pyramids placed base-to-base

ONYX: A mineral mass featuring parallel bands of a mineral, particularly chalcedony (quartz) or calcite

OPAQUE: Material that lets no light through

ORE: Rocks or minerals from which metals can be extracted

OXIDATION: The process of a metal or mineral combining with oxygen, which can produce new colors or minerals

PEARLY: A mineral with reflectivity resembling that of a pearl

PEGMATITE: The lowest portion of a granite formation, where the minerals within the magma are allowed great amounts of time to cool and therefore fully crystallize, often resulting in very large, and sometimes rare, crystals

PHENOCRYST: A crystal embedded within igneous rock that solidified before the rest of the surrounding rock, thus retaining its true crystal shape

PHOSPHORESCENCE: Fluorescent minerals that continue to emit light after a radiation source has been removed

PLACER: Deposit of sand containing dense, heavy mineral grains at the bottom of a river or lake

POLYMORPH: Chemical compounds that crystallize in different forms depending on the environmental conditions during formation. For instance, titanium dioxide can form three distinct materials: rutile, brookite, or anatase

PORPHYRY: An igneous rock containing many phenocrysts

PRIMARY: An original formation of rock

PRISMATIC: Crystals with a length greater than their width and at least four sides of similar length and width

PSEUDOMORPH: When one mineral replaces another but retains the outward appearance of the initial mineral

PYRAMIDAL: Crystals resembling a pyramid with four or more total faces

PYROXENE: A group of dark, rock-building minerals that make up many dark-colored rock like basalt or gabbro

RADIATING: Crystal aggregates growing outward from a central point, resembling the shape of a paper fan

REGIONAL METAMORPHISM: Metamorphosis occurring in a large amount of rock as a result of great heat and pressure over a large area

RHOMBOHEDRON: A four-sided shape resembling a tilted or leaning cube

ROCK: A massive aggregate of mineral grains

ROCK-FORMING: Refers to a mineral important in rock creation

SCHIST: A rock that has been metamorphosed so that most of its minerals have been concentrated and arranged into parallel layers

SECONDARY: A rock or mineral that formed later than the rock surrounding it

SEDIMENT: Fine particles of rocks or minerals deposited by water or wind, e.g., sand

SEDIMENTARY ROCK: Rock derived from sediment being cemented together

SERIES: A small group of minerals with nearly identical chemical compounds wherein one element can interchange with another and retain the same molecular structure, e.g., $FeWO_4$ is in series with $MnWO_4$ and both create similar minerals

SERPENTINE: A group of iron- and magnesium-rich minerals that are generally green in color with a greasy texture

SILICA: Silicon dioxide, more commonly known as quartz

SMELTING: Processing a rock or mineral, usually by melting, in order to separate metals

SOAPSTONE: A metamorphic rock consisting primarily of talc, an extremely soft mineral that feels slippery and resembles soap

SODA: Sodium carbonate; a chemical compound containing sodium and carbon. Often used to describe sodium-rich compounds or minerals

SPECIFIC GRAVITY: The ratio of the density of a given solid or liquid to the density of water e.g., the specific gravity of galena is approximately 7.5, meaning that a sample of galena is about 7.5 times heavier than the same amount of water

SPECIMEN: A sample of a rock or mineral

STALACTITIC: Resembling a stalactite, which is a cone-shaped mineral deposit; carrot-shaped

STRIATED: Parallel grooves in the surface of a mineral

TABULAR: A crystal structure in which one dimension is notably shorter than the others, resulting in flat, plate-like shapes

TARNISH: A thin coating on the surface of a metal, often differently colored from the metal itself (see *oxidation*)

TRANSLUCENT: A material that lets some light through

TRANSPARENT: A material that lets enough light through as to be able to see what lies on the other side

TWIN: An intergrowth of two or more crystals

TYPE LOCALITY: The location where a particular mineral was first discovered and described

TYPE-LOCALITY SPECIMEN: A mineral specimen collected from the site where that mineral was originally discovered and described. For example, the mineral bixbyite was first discovered in the Thomas Range, Utah; therefore, any sample of bixbyite from that location is a type-locality specimen

VEIN: A mineral, particularly a metal, that has filled a crack or similar opening in a host rock or mineral

VESICLE: A rounded cavity created in an igneous rock by a gas bubble trapped when the rock solidified

VESICULAR: Containing many vesicles; a rock containing vesicles is said to be vesicular

VITREOUS: A mineral with a reflectivity resembling that of glass

VUG: A small irregular cavity within a rock or mineral that can become lined with different crystals.

WAXY: A mineral with a reflectivity resembling that of wax, such as a candle

ZEOLITE: A complex group of minerals that contain aluminum, silica and excess water. Their water content can be lost and regained easily

Recommended Reading

Bates, Robert L., editor, *Dictionary of Geological Terms, 3rd Edition*. New York: Anchor Books, 1984.

Bonewitz, Ronald Louis, *Smithsonian Rock and Gem*. New York: DK Publishing, 2005.

Chesteman, Charles W., *The Audubon Society Field Guide to North American Rocks and Minerals*. New York: Knopf, 1979.

Johnsen, Ole, *Minerals of the World*. New Jersey: Princeton University Press, 2004.

Mottana, Annibale, et al. *Simon and Schuster's Guide to Rocks and Minerals*. New York: Simon and Schuster, 1978.

Pellant, Chris, *Rocks and Minerals*. New York: Dorling Kindersley Publishing, 2002.

Pough, Frederick H., *Rocks and Minerals*. Boston: Houghton Mifflin, 1988.

About the Author

Dan R. Lynch has a degree in graphic design with emphasis on photography from the University of Minnesota Duluth. However, before his love of the arts, he developed a passion for rocks, minerals and fossils while growing up at his parents' rock shop, Agate City. Combining the two aspects of his life seemed a natural choice and he enjoys both writing about and taking photographs of minerals. Working with his father, Bob Lynch, a respected veteran of the Minnesota rock-collecting community, Dan spearheads their series of rock and mineral field guides. This logbook is his first solo effort and he is proud to present his close-up mineral photography to the public for the first time. He currently lives the comfortable life of a writer in Duluth, Minnesota, with his beautiful fiancée, Julie.

CPSIA information can be obtained
at www.ICGtesting.com
Printed in the USA
JSHW020513300722
28599JS00006BB/6